JAMAR NICHOLAS'

LEON ™

Protector of the Playground

Story and Art by Jamar Nicholas Studios, in
conjunction with the Comic Book Diner Partnership

jamarnicholas.com

LEON

Protector of the Playground

Created, Written, and Illustrated
by

Jamar Nicholas

Additional Art, Colors & Letters by

Raen Ngu

Book Design by
John Gallagher

Schedule of Events:

Extra Credit

I dedicate this book
to the memory of my mother,
Eula Nicholas, my hero.

Part 1

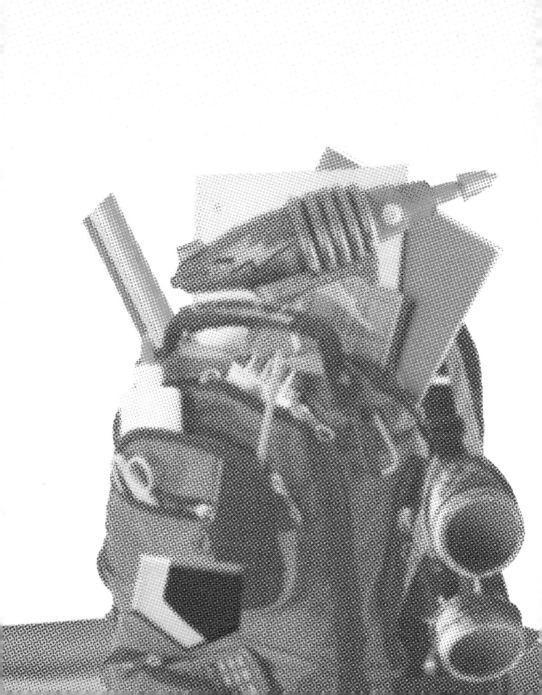

9

Part 2

LATER, AFTER LUNCH, AND BEFORE THAT PAINFUL LAST 15 MINUTES OF SCHOOL . . .

WELCOME TO
GUILLAUME ELEMENTARY
HOME OF THE FIGHTIN' PIGEONS

ALRIGHT CLASS, I HOPE YOU DIDN'T FORGET TO BRING IN ITEMS TO DISCUSS FROM SUMMER VACATION.

OBOY! I CAN'T WAIT TO TALK ABOUT ICE ART!

OVER THE SUMMER, I WON MY GOLDFISH, BRUCE, AT THE FAIR. HE KNOWS HOW TO FLOAT UPSIDE-DOWN REAL GOOD.

I BROUGHT IN MY FROG, MILQUETOAST. HE EATS FLIES, OAT-MEAL, AND GUMMY BEARS.

THIS IS A DARKMATTER CUBE, FROM THE 10TH DIMENSION OF SHADOW-SPACE. I GOT THIS AND A T-SHIRT ON VACATION WITH MY MOM.

Part 3

AFTER-SCHOOL, LEON VISITS A FAMILY FRIEND FOR TUTORING AND *TREATS!*

KRUNK'S Bakery

DA-DING! DA-DING!

YO! MS. KRUNK! I'M HERE TO SAVE THE--

Key Lime Pie
Rhubarb Pie
St...

Coffee & Cake Special

WHOOPIE PIE 1 doz.

CAKES AND PIES... MMMM!

HI LEON! ALWAYS ON TIME. IS *CARLOS* WITH YOU?

44

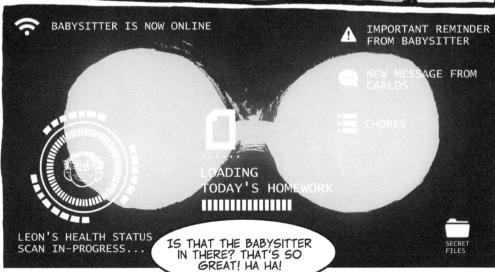

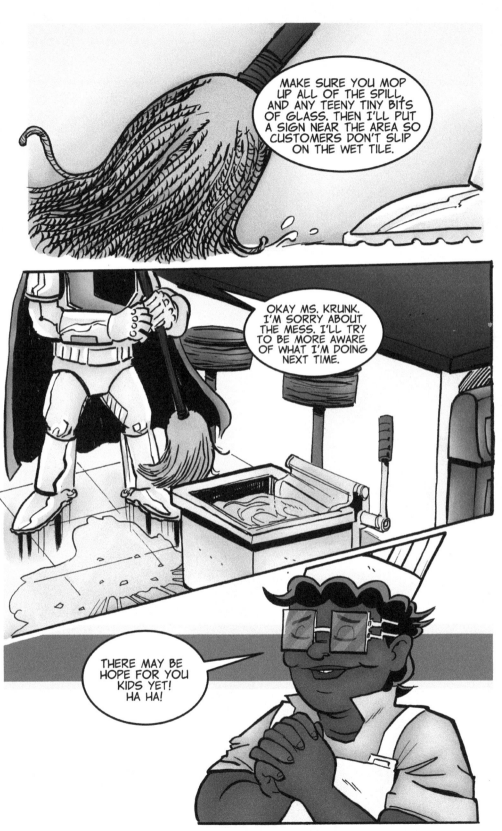

KLIK

KLIKACK

PLAY CLOTHES
CASUAL COSTUME 2.0
MISTER MAGNIFICENT LOADOUT

ZIP!

1 2 3

I LOVE
THIS
PART!

OKAY, WILL YOU PLEASE TAP INTO ANY BULLY CHATTER?

THAT'S BETTER. SCANNING/ / / THERE IS ACTIVITY AT THE SFV TREEHOUSE.

WELL, THE MONOCLE DID HAVE TO ATTEND HOME-SUMMER SCHOOL AND BLAMES YOU. HE AND THE -- ALERT! ALERT!

THEY NEVER GIVE UP. WHAT'S THEIR DEAL? STILL MAD AT ME ABOUT 5TH GRADE?

DING-DONG!

SCANNING/ / / CARLOS KRUNK IS AT DOCK DOOR 5020.

OKAY. TURN OFF THE LASERS. PLEASE.

THEY SEEM TO BE PLOTTING A CAPER, LEON.

I HAVE SOME CONVERSATION BEFORE A LOUD SOUND STOPS IT.

HEY, COOL! LEMME LISTEN, LEON!

YOU DON'T EVEN HAVE EARS IN THAT COSTUME. JUST CHILL OUT, SO I CAN HEAR WHAT THEY'RE SAYING.

WEIRD. THERE'S A VOICE THAT SAID "FREON" THEN A LOT OF SCREAMS . . .

THAT'S NOT A SCARY WORD. I WOULDN'T SCREAM FOR THAT. UNLESS IT WAS A SPIDER. YO, I'D SCREAM IF IT WAS A SPIDER!

NOT SURE WHAT THEY'RE PLANNING, BUT I SHOULD BE READY FOR WHATEVER THEY HAVE FOR ME.

ESPECIALLY THIS FREON THING. IF THAT SCARED THEM, THAT CAN'T BE GOOD FOR ME.

ESPECIALLY IF FREON IS THE SPIDER'S NAME! OH MAN, SPIDERS GIVE ME THE JIMMIES!

Part 4

A FEW DAYS LATER

WELCOME TO
GUILLAUME ELEMENTARY
FISH STICK FRIDAY
BRING YOUR OWN TARTAR SAUCE

THANKS FOR COMING, MRS. OLDHEAD!

THE STUDENTS ARE GOING TO LOVE HEARING YOU TALK AT OUR *CAREER DAY* ASSEMBLY TODAY!

CONSIDERING YOU HAVEN'T SAID MUCH SINCE YOU'VE BEEN HERE! I GUESS YOU'RE SAVING IT FOR THE KIDS, RIGHT?

...

68

Part 5

93

I THOUGHT AFTER MRS. OLDHEAD TALKS, WE'D TALK TO SIGNE WILKINSON ABOUT BEING A PROFESSIONAL CARTOONIST!

ART IS A SUPER POWER!

THEN WE'LL HAVE GARY YAP,

LYNN KRUNK,

MICKEY CHEEK!

AND LAST BUT NOT LEAST, CAPTAIN TEMERITY AND STORMCHASER ...

SO HOW MUCH DO WE GET PAID FOR THIS?

THERE YOU ARE.

LOOKS LIKE YOU'VE BEEN BUSY. I DON'T KNOW WHY YOU'RE SITTING AT MY DESK, BUT I KNOW THAT YOU CAN'T STAY HERE ANY LONGER.

I KNOW NOW THAT IT WAS IRRESPONSIBLE TO BRING THAT CUBE TO SCHOOL. IT'S MY FAULT YOU'RE HERE. NOT CLEMS.

SHMMMMMMMMMMMMMMMMMMMMMMMMMMMMM

FREEEE ONNNNN!

EVEN THOUGH I'M JUST A KID, I FELT LIKE I WAS IN CHARGE OF PROTECTING A WHOLE SCHOOL. MORE THAN JUST A PLAYGROUND.

THAT'S A LOT. EVEN THOUGH I DIDN'T SEE IT, I HAD FRIENDS THAT WANTED TO HELP, BUT I NEVER LET THEM. I FELT LIKE I HAD TO DO IT ALL BY MYSELF.

BUT I DON'T HAVE TO.

I'M LOOKING FORWARD TO MY NEXT ADVENTURE, WHERE I KNOW I CAN ASK FOR HELP IF I NEED IT.

AND THAT IS REALLY MAGNIFICENT!

PAUSED

SO, WHAT DID YOU THINK?

HEY GUYS! IT'S ME, CHALMERS AGAIN! WHAT A GREAT ADVENTURE! I'M EXCITED TO SEE WHAT HAPPENS TOMORROW, THOUGH EVERYBODY'S WORRIED ABOUT PRINCIPAL PRINCIPLE, I'M SURE LEON WILL FIGURE THAT OUT TOO. . . AND IF HE CAN'T, HIS FRIENDS WILL HELP.

EVERY DAY IS EPIC WHEN LEON IS YOUR BEST BUD!

● REC

AND I'LL BE HERE EVERY TIME TO GIVE YOU THE STREAMING PLAY BY PLAY!

● REC

CHALMERS! WHAT ARE YOU DOING OVER THERE?!

OHNO, BUSTED!

THIS IS THE END, YOUNG MAN.

⇌URK!⇌ MS. CORNOG! I WAS JUST--

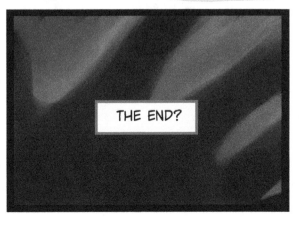

THE END?

Epilogue

ALSO RHAZMRGRAFS, MY FAVORITE KIND OF RHAZM!

Math, art, science, hall passes-- Dimension X has it all...

215

...Even heroes.

TMP.

The Great Broccolini

MISTER NIPSEY:
(1 THROUGH 14)

THE SHORT-LIVED HYPER-INTELLIGENT HAMSTERS WHO HAVE BEEN PETS OF THE MONOCLE, ARE USUALLY THE BRAINS BEHIND MONOCLE'S TECHNOLOGY. NIPSEY CAN BE SPOTTED PILOTING A WALKING ROBOT HABITRAIL.

THE MONOCLE:

THADDEUS MONOCLE III, ONE IN A LONG LINE OF CYCLOPES, CONSPIRES TO DEFEAT LEON AND HAS FORMED THE STEEPLE-FINGERED VILLAINS TO AID HIM IN THIS.

UNCLE EYESORE

THE TATTLESNAKE:

ARNOLD BENEDICT MUTATED INTO A COLD-BLOODED TATTLER AND HAS EVER SINCE BEEN A KNOWN INFOR-MATION GATHERER FOR THE MONOCLE. DON'T TRUST HIM WITH SECRETS.

THE TARDY BOYS:

A GROUP OF UN-SUPER STUDENTS, HAVE BEEN IN DETENTION SO LONG, THEIR SKIN HAS TURNED PALE. THEY BLAME LEON FOR THEIR DETENTION SENTENCE.

BROCCOLI ROB:

SEE ORIGIN DOCUMENT ATTACHED.

BRAHMA BULLY:

REAL NAME UNKNOWN, POSSESSES REMARKABLE STRENGTH AND ATTACKS WHEN HE IS PROVOKED OR SEES THE COLOR RED. HE SECRETLY IS A FAN OF LEON BUT DOESN'T WANT TO UPSET THE MONOCLE WITH THIS INFORMATION.

FREON:
COLD COUSIN

A CURIOUS CASE FOR LEON, FREON WAS CONSTRUCTED FROM DARKMATTER ENERGY AND CHALMER'S ICE SCULPTURE. CAN GENERATE AND CONTROL COLD AND ICE. NOTES BELIEVE HE MAY BE A DIMENSIONAL ALTERNATE OF LEON.

UNCONFIRMED

CLEMENTINE JUSTICE:

CLEMENTINE IS DAUGHTER OF SUPER-MARRIED TEAM, JUSTICE AND PEACE, AND EXHIBITS MORPHING ABILITIES TIED TO HER EMOTIONAL STATE. STRONG-WILLED, CLEM HAS AN ARMY OF HALL MONITOR MINIONS AT HER CALL TO DO HER BIDDING.

PRINCIPAL PRINCIPLE:

GLENN GEOFFREY PRINCIPLE HAS BEEN IN CHARGE OF GUILLAUME SCHOOL FOR YEARS, BUT HAS A MYSTERIOUS BACKGROUND. REPORTS RUMOR THAT HE MAY HAVE BEEN THE SUPER-CRIMEFIGHTER THE EDUCATOR, BUT IT HASN'T BEEN PROVEN.

LYNN KRUNK:

MOTHER OF LEON'S BEST FRIEND CARLOS, MS. KRUNK WAS PART OF THE SUPER-TRIO, BUTCHER, BAKER AND CANDLESTICK MAKER, BUT RETIRED TO OPEN A STORE AND RAISE HER SON. SHE AND LEON'S MOTHER ARE ALSO BEST FRIENDS.

CARLOS KRUNK:

CARLOS IS LEON'S BEST BUD AND ALSO LOVES DRAWING CARTOONS, IF HE EVER GETS OUT OF THAT PIGEON COSTUME.

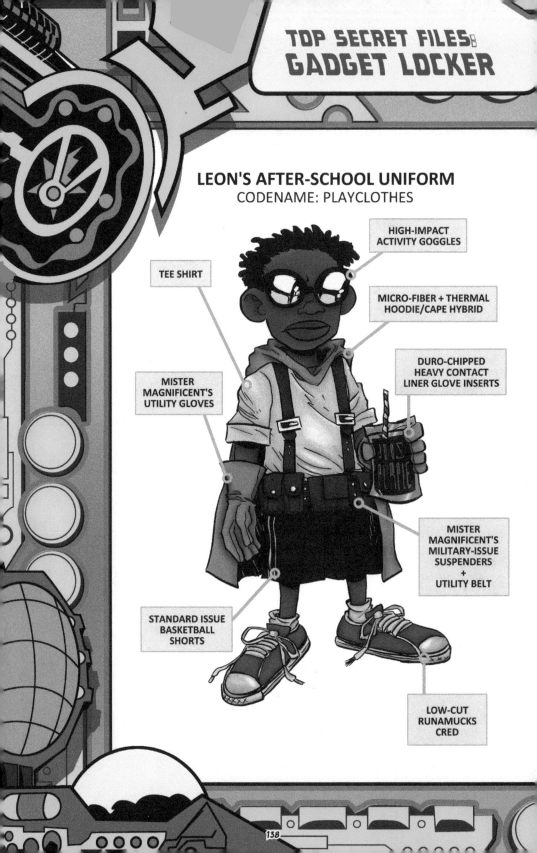

TOP SECRET FILES:
GADGET LOCKER

LEON'S AFTER-SCHOOL UNIFORM
CODENAME: PLAYCLOTHES

HIGH-IMPACT ACTIVITY GOGGLES

TEE SHIRT

MICRO-FIBER + THERMAL HOODIE/CAPE HYBRID

DURO-CHIPPED HEAVY CONTACT LINER GLOVE INSERTS

MISTER MAGNIFICENT'S UTILITY GLOVES

MISTER MAGNIFICENT'S MILITARY-ISSUE SUSPENDERS + UTILITY BELT

STANDARD ISSUE BASKETBALL SHORTS

LOW-CUT RUNAMUCKS CRED

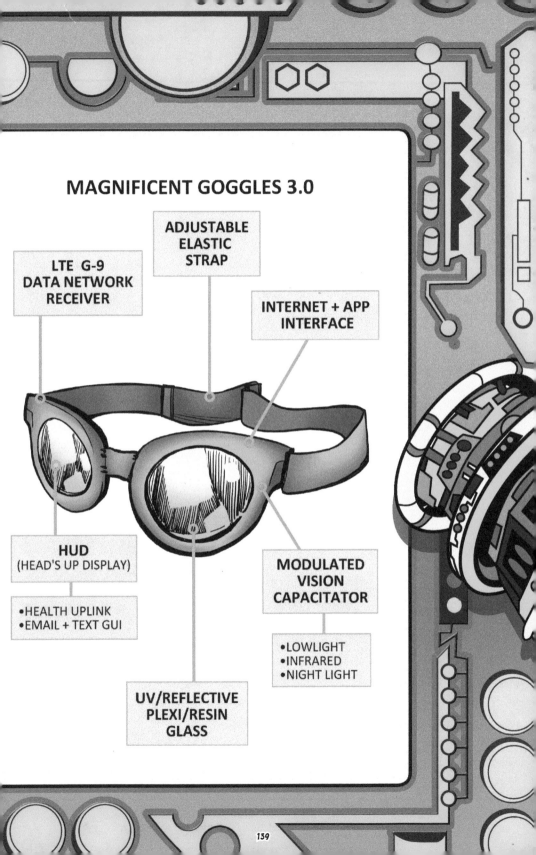

MAGNIFICENT GOGGLES 3.0

ADJUSTABLE ELASTIC STRAP

LTE G-9 DATA NETWORK RECEIVER

INTERNET + APP INTERFACE

HUD
(HEAD'S UP DISPLAY)

•HEALTH UPLINK
•EMAIL + TEXT GUI

MODULATED VISION CAPACITATOR

•LOWLIGHT
•INFRARED
•NIGHT LIGHT

UV/REFLECTIVE PLEXI/RESIN GLASS

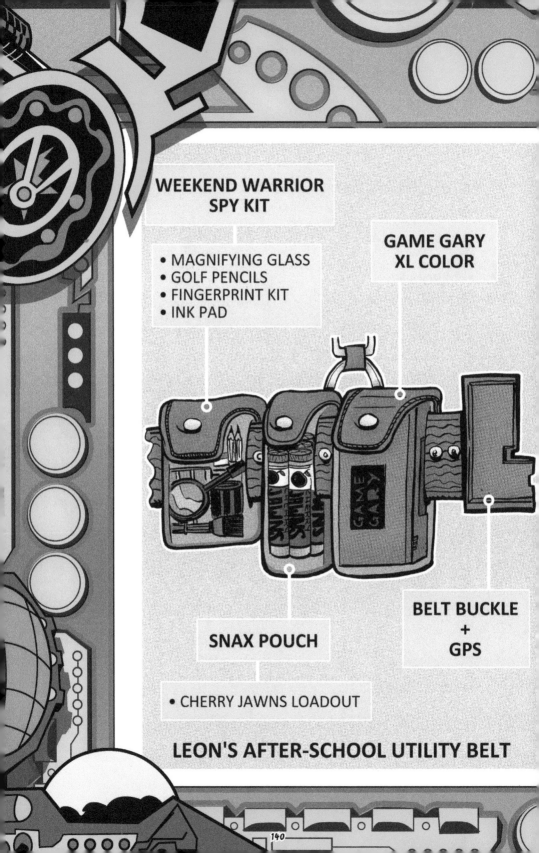

WEEKEND WARRIOR SPY KIT

- MAGNIFYING GLASS
- GOLF PENCILS
- FINGERPRINT KIT
- INK PAD

GAME GARY XL COLOR

SNAX POUCH

- CHERRY JAWNS LOADOUT

BELT BUCKLE + GPS

LEON'S AFTER-SCHOOL UTILITY BELT

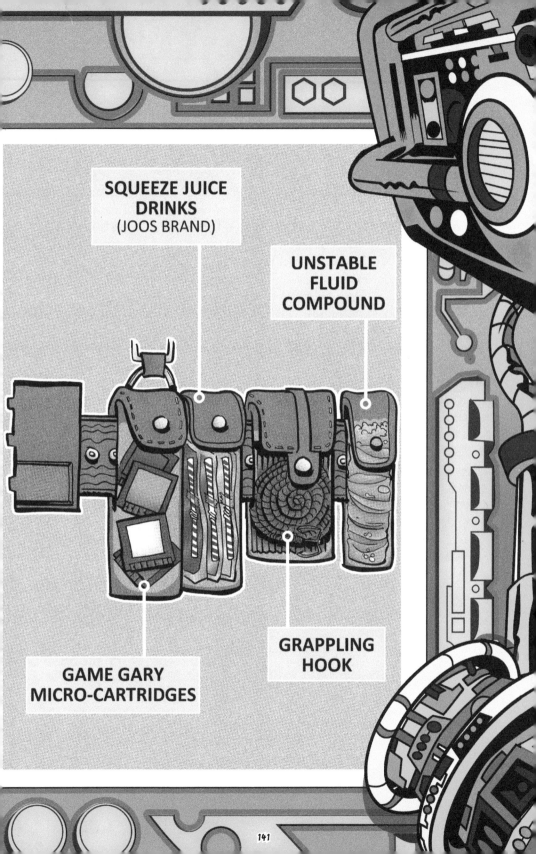

SQUEEZE JUICE
DRINKS
(JOOS BRAND)

UNSTABLE
FLUID
COMPOUND

GAME GARY
MICRO-CARTRIDGES

GRAPPLING
HOOK

Honor Roll

Thank you to our Kickstarter Supporters

Trey Alexander
Samax Amen
(GhettoManga Quarterly)
Derek Anderson
Lisa Anderson
Vince Bayless
Leonard Beish
Omar Bilal
Robin Bono
Jason Brashier
John Broglia
James Brown
Joel Castor
Alisha M Cheek (Mickey)
Carlos Cheek
Mike Clarke
Beth & Jonathan Cohen
John Collins
(Johnny Splendor)
Lamont Connor
Martha Cornog
Colleen Crowley
Mishael Devlin
Dave DeVries

Brandon Eaker
Josh Elder
Greg McElhatton
David Elliott
Tony Esteves
Adrienne Faber
Andrew Fernandes
Stephen Fluhr
David Fogelman
Lisa Fortuner
Jason Fusco
Pawel Goj
Jason Hart
Ben Harvey
Tabitha Hendershot
Dave Housley
Michael Howard
Josh Howell
Amy Ignatow
Kelly Ishikawa
Gwenaël Jacquet
ProfJonathan

Katharine Kan
Stu Kesilman
Patty Kirsch
Nikka & Jon Landau
Dann Leccese
Ryan Lee
A. David Lewis
Walter Mahoski
Mark Mariano
Christian McCloskey
Justin McGill
Liz McMahon
Chad Merritt
Bjorn Munson
Joe Murray
Bruce Nelson
Kerry O'Connor
(krossoconnor)
Kathleen O'Hearn
Jerry Ordway
Andrea Pandolfi
Michael Penick
Blake Petit
Oscar Pinto
Roy Quini

Rob Reilly
Michael Rhode
Rafer Roberts
Christina Rogers
Ellen Ruby
Anthony Ruttgaizer
(Anthony Kingdom
James)
Abbey Ryan
Chris Sama
Charles Sarratt
Scott Christian Sava
Lois Scavone
schiff (shepard)
Stephen Schlosser
Britt Schramm
David Schwartz
Corey Christian Scott
Dorothea Stahl
Tom Stillwell
Greg Stoll
Joshua Stone
Patrick Michael Strange
Bobby Timony
J. Torres
Bradford Tree
Robert & Cheryl Turk
Signe Wilkinson
Jennifer Praul
Winterscheidt
Gary Yap
(ArtOverLifeStudios)
Thomas Zahler
Chris Zechman
James Zintel

Thanks!

Special thanks go to Darcy, for everything.

To Sandra, for her tireless assistance; to my Comic Book Diner brothers—Rich and John; Mike Manley for inking help and being an artistic beacon in the darkness. The Super Mariano Brothers—Chris and Mark for your passion and positivity; To The Grahamatow family; Eric Nolen-Weathington for your early support and advice; Nicholas Waters IV and family; kris and JD; Mike Hawthorne and family; Samax Amen for his energy and love of the project early on; To Steve Conley and Thom Zahler—thanks for being on standby life-support; Tom Whitefield, with my Magnificent thanks. Also thanks to the Kickstarter backers for the support and taking a chance on something new.

And to the rest of my friends, family, and anyone else who patiently cheered me on while I ran this race, thank you.

About the Author

JAMAR NICHOLAS is an award-winning, Philadelphia-based artist and educator. He has taught and lectured on the topic of comics creation at numerous institutions, dedicating his career to empowering young people to create their own cartoons and comics, helping them realize the power of visual narrative.

Some of his works include illustrating Annie Auerbach's chapterbook series THE GROSSE ADVENTURES (Tokyopop), adapting and illustrating Geoffrey Canada's memoir FIST STICK KNIFE GUN as well as prodcuing his full-color daily comic strip, DETECTIVE BOOGALOO: HIP HOP COP, that was serialized in the US Metro newspapers (Philadelphia, NYC and Boston).

He is also a writer and columnist for DRAW! Magazine, the How-To source for comic book and animation professionals, as well as a host of the COMIC BOOK DINER podcast, focusing on the business of comics.